Leap Of Faith

"Today, I've decided to step out on faith and leave the results to You."

Leap Of Faith

"Today, I've decided to step out on faith and leave the results to You."

Leap Of Faith

"Today, I've decided to step out on faith and leave the results to You."

Leap Of Faith

"Today, I've decided to step out on faith and leave the results to You."

Leap Of Faith

"Today, I've decided to step out on faith and leave the results to You."

Leap Of Faith

"Today, I've decided to step out on faith and leave the results to You."

Leap Of Faith

"Today, I've decided to step out on faith and leave the results to You."

Leap Of Faith

"Today, I've decided to step out on faith and leave the results to You."

Leap Of Faith

"Today, I've decided to step out on faith and leave the results to You."

Leap Of Faith

"Today, I've decided to step out on faith and leave the results to You."

Leap Of Faith

"Today, I've decided to step out on faith and leave the results to You."

Leap Of Faith

"Today, I've decided to step out on faith and leave the results to You."

Leap Of Faith

"Today, I've decided to step out on faith and leave the results to You."

Leap Of Faith

"Today, I've decided to step out on faith and leave the results to You."

Leap Of Faith

"Today, I've decided to step out on faith and leave the results to You."

Leap Of Faith

"Today, I've decided to step out on faith and leave the results to You."

Leap Of Faith

"Today, I've decided to step out on faith and leave the results to You."

Leap Of Faith

"Today, I've decided to step out on faith and leave the results to You."

Leap Of Faith

"Today, I've decided to step out on faith and leave the results to You."

Leap Of Faith

"Today, I've decided to step out on faith and leave the results to You."

Leap Of Faith

"Today, I've decided to step out on faith and leave the results to You."

Leap Of Faith

"Today, I've decided to step out on faith and leave the results to You."

Leap Of Faith

"Today, I've decided to step out on faith and leave the results to You."

Leap Of Faith

"Today, I've decided to step out on faith and leave the results to You."

Leap Of Faith

"Today, I've decided to step out on faith and leave the results to You."

Leap Of Faith

"Today, I've decided to step out on faith and leave the results to You."

Leap Of Faith

"Today, I've decided to step out on faith and leave the results to You."

Leap Of Faith

"Today, I've decided to step out on faith and leave the results to You."

Leap Of Faith

"Today, I've decided to step out on faith and leave the results to You."

Leap Of Faith

"Today, I've decided to step out on faith and leave the results to You."

Leap Of Faith

"Today, I've decided to step out on faith and leave the results to You."

Leap Of Faith

"Today, I've decided to step out on faith and leave the results to You."

Leap Of Faith

"Today, I've decided to step out on faith and leave the results to You."

Leap Of Faith

"Today, I've decided to step out on faith and leave the results to You."

Leap Of Faith

"Today, I've decided to step out on faith and leave the results to You."

Leap Of Faith

"Today, I've decided to step out on faith and leave the results to You."

Leap Of Faith

"Today, I've decided to step out on faith and leave the results to You."

Leap Of Faith

"Today, I've decided to step out on faith and leave the results to You."

Leap Of Faith

"Today, I've decided to step out on faith and leave the results to You."

Leap Of Faith

"Today, I've decided to step out on faith and leave the results to You."

Leap Of Faith

"Today, I've decided to step out on faith and leave the results to You."

Leap Of Faith

"Today, I've decided to step out on faith and leave the results to You."

Leap Of Faith

"Today, I've decided to step out on faith and leave the results to You."

Leap Of Faith

"Today, I've decided to step out on faith and leave the results to You."

Leap Of Faith

"Today, I've decided to step out on faith and leave the results to You."

Leap Of Faith

"Today, I've decided to step out on faith and leave the results to You."

Leap Of Faith

"Today, I've decided to step out on faith and leave the results to You."

Leap Of Faith

"Today, I've decided to step out on faith and leave the results to You."

Leap Of Faith

"Today, I've decided to step out on faith and leave the results to You."

Leap Of Faith

"Today, I've decided to step out on faith and leave the results to You."

Leap Of Faith

"Today, I've decided to step out on faith and leave the results to You."

Leap Of Faith

"Today, I've decided to step out on faith and leave the results to You."

Leap Of Faith

"Today, I've decided to step out on faith and leave the results to You."

Leap Of Faith

"Today, I've decided to step out on faith and leave the results to You."

Leap Of Faith

"Today, I've decided to step out on faith and leave the results to You."

Leap Of Faith

"Today, I've decided to step out on faith and leave the results to You."

Leap Of Faith

"Today, I've decided to step out on faith and leave the results to You."

Leap Of Faith

"Today, I've decided to step out on faith and leave the results to You."

Leap Of Faith

"Today, I've decided to step out on faith and leave the results to You."

Leap Of Faith

"Today, I've decided to step out on faith and leave the results to You."

Leap Of Faith

"Today, I've decided to step out on faith and leave the results to You."

Leap Of Faith

"Today, I've decided to step out on faith and leave the results to You."

Leap Of Faith

"Today, I've decided to step out on faith and leave the results to You."

Leap Of Faith

"Today, I've decided to step out on faith and leave the results to You."

Leap Of Faith

"Today, I've decided to step out on faith and leave the results to You."

Leap Of Faith

"Today, I've decided to step out on faith and leave the results to You."

Leap Of Faith

"Today, I've decided to step out on faith and leave the results to You."

Leap Of Faith

"Today, I've decided to step out on faith and leave the results to You."

Leap Of Faith

"Today, I've decided to step out on faith and leave the results to You."

Leap Of Faith

"Today, I've decided to step out on faith and leave the results to You."

Leap Of Faith

"Today, I've decided to step out on faith and leave the results to You."

Leap Of Faith

"Today, I've decided to step out on faith and leave the results to You."

Leap Of Faith

"Today, I've decided to step out on faith and leave the results to You."

Leap Of Faith

"Today, I've decided to step out on faith and leave the results to You."

Leap Of Faith

"Today, I've decided to step out on faith and leave the results to You."

Leap Of Faith

"Today, I've decided to step out on faith and leave the results to You."

Leap Of Faith

"Today, I've decided to step out on faith and leave the results to You."

Leap Of Faith

"Today, I've decided to step out on faith and leave the results to You."

Leap Of Faith

"Today, I've decided to step out on faith and leave the results to You."

Leap Of Faith

"Today, I've decided to step out on faith and leave the results to You."

Leap Of Faith

"Today, I've decided to step out on faith and leave the results to You."

Leap Of Faith

"Today, I've decided to step out on faith and leave the results to You."

Leap Of Faith

"Today, I've decided to step out on faith and leave the results to You."

Leap Of Faith

"Today, I've decided to step out on faith and leave the results to You."

Leap Of Faith

"Today, I've decided to step out on faith and leave the results to You."

Leap Of Faith

"Today, I've decided to step out on faith and leave the results to You."

Leap Of Faith

"Today, I've decided to step out on faith and leave the results to You."

Leap Of Faith

"Today, I've decided to step out on faith and leave the results to You."

Leap Of Faith

"Today, I've decided to step out on faith and leave the results to You."

Leap Of Faith

"Today, I've decided to step out on faith and leave the results to You."

Leap Of Faith

"Today, I've decided to step out on faith and leave the results to You."

Leap Of Faith

"Today, I've decided to step out on faith and leave the results to You."

Leap Of Faith

"Today, I've decided to step out on faith and leave the results to You."

Leap Of Faith

"Today, I've decided to step out on faith and leave the results to You."

Leap Of Faith

"Today, I've decided to step out on faith and leave the results to You."

Leap Of Faith

"Today, I've decided to step out on faith and leave the results to You."

Leap Of Faith

"Today, I've decided to step out on faith and leave the results to You."

Leap Of Faith

"Today, I've decided to step out on faith and leave the results to You."

Leap Of Faith

"Today, I've decided to step out on faith and leave the results to You."

Leap Of Faith

"Today, I've decided to step out on faith and leave the results to You."

Leap Of Faith

"Today, I've decided to step out on faith and leave the results to You."

Leap Of Faith

"Today, I've decided to step out on faith and leave the results to You."

Leap Of Faith

"Today, I've decided to step out on faith and leave the results to You."

Leap Of Faith

"Today, I've decided to step out on faith and leave the results to You."

Leap Of Faith

"Today, I've decided to step out on faith and leave the results to You."

Leap Of Faith

"Today, I've decided to step out on faith and leave the results to You."

Leap Of Faith

"Today, I've decided to step out on faith and leave the results to You."

Leap Of Faith

"Today, I've decided to step out on faith and leave the results to You."

Leap Of Faith

"Today, I've decided to step out on faith and leave the results to You."

Leap Of Faith

"Today, I've decided to step out on faith and leave the results to You."

Leap Of Faith

"Today, I've decided to step out on faith and leave the results to You."

Leap Of Faith

"Today, I've decided to step out on faith and leave the results to You."

Leap Of Faith

"Today, I've decided to step out on faith and leave the results to You."

Leap Of Faith

"Today, I've decided to step out on faith and leave the results to You."

Leap Of Faith

"Today, I've decided to step out on faith and leave the results to You."

Leap Of Faith

"Today, I've decided to step out on faith and leave the results to You."

Leap Of Faith

_____

_____

_____

_____

_____

_____

_____

_____

_____

_____

_____

_____

_____

_____

_____

_____

_____

_____

_____

_____

_____

_____

"Today, I've decided to step out on faith and leave the results to You."

Leap Of Faith

"Today, I've decided to step out on faith and leave the results to You."

Leap Of Faith

"Today, I've decided to step out on faith and leave the results to You."

Leap Of Faith

"Today, I've decided to step out on faith and leave the results to You."

Leap Of Faith

"Today, I've decided to step out on faith and leave the results to You."

Leap Of Faith

"Today, I've decided to step out on faith and leave the results to You."

Leap Of Faith

"Today, I've decided to step out on faith and leave the results to You."

Leap Of Faith

"Today, I've decided to step out on faith and leave the results to You."

Leap Of Faith

"Today, I've decided to step out on faith and leave the results to You."

Leap Of Faith

"Today, I've decided to step out on faith and leave the results to You."

Leap Of Faith

"Today, I've decided to step out on faith and leave the results to You."

Leap Of Faith

"Today, I've decided to step out on faith and leave the results to You."

Leap Of Faith

"Today, I've decided to step out on faith and leave the results to You."

Leap Of Faith

"Today, I've decided to step out on faith and leave the results to You."

Leap Of Faith

"Today, I've decided to step out on faith and leave the results to You."

Leap Of Faith

"Today, I've decided to step out on faith and leave the results to You."

Leap Of Faith

"Today, I've decided to step out on faith and leave the results to You."

Leap Of Faith

"Today, I've decided to step out on faith and leave the results to You."

Leap Of Faith

"Today, I've decided to step out on faith and leave the results to You."

Leap Of Faith

"Today, I've decided to step out on faith and leave the results to You."

Leap Of Faith

"Today, I've decided to step out on faith and leave the results to You."

Leap Of Faith

"Today, I've decided to step out on faith and leave the results to You."

Leap Of Faith

"Today, I've decided to step out on faith and leave the results to You."

Leap Of Faith

"Today, I've decided to step out on faith and leave the results to You."

Leap Of Faith

"Today, I've decided to step out on faith and leave the results to You."

Leap Of Faith

"Today, I've decided to step out on faith and leave the results to You."

Leap Of Faith

"Today, I've decided to step out on faith and leave the results to You."

Leap Of Faith

"Today, I've decided to step out on faith and leave the results to You."

Leap Of Faith

"Today, I've decided to step out on faith and leave the results to You."

Leap Of Faith

"Today, I've decided to step out on faith and leave the results to You."

Leap Of Faith

"Today, I've decided to step out on faith and leave the results to You."

Leap Of Faith

"Today, I've decided to step out on faith and leave the results to You."

Leap Of Faith

"Today, I've decided to step out on faith and leave the results to You."

Leap Of Faith

"Today, I've decided to step out on faith and leave the results to You."

Leap Of Faith

"Today, I've decided to step out on faith and leave the results to You."

Leap Of Faith

"Today, I've decided to step out on faith and leave the results to You."

Leap Of Faith

"Today, I've decided to step out on faith and leave the results to You."

Leap Of Faith

"Today, I've decided to step out on faith and leave the results to You."

Leap Of Faith

"Today, I've decided to step out on faith and leave the results to You."

Leap Of Faith

"Today, I've decided to step out on faith and leave the results to You."

Leap Of Faith

"Today, I've decided to step out on faith and leave the results to You."

Leap Of Faith

"Today, I've decided to step out on faith and leave the results to You."

Leap Of Faith

"Today, I've decided to step out on faith and leave the results to You."